All Rain, No Mud

SIMPLE SECRETS FOR HAPPINESS . . . EVEN ON RAINY DAYS

SHARON LARSEN

DESERET
BOOK

SALT LAKE CITY, UTAH

Library of Congress Cataloging-in-Publication Data

Larsen, Sharon G.

   All rain, no mud / Sharon Larsen.

    p.   cm.

   ISBN 1-59038-484-9 (hardbound : alk. paper)

    1. Christian life—Mormon authors.   2. Christian women—Religious life.

3. Larsen, Sharon G.   4. Mormons—Biography.   I. Title.

   BX8656.L38   2005

   289.3'092—dc22   2005013299

Printed in Canada   29359

Friesens, Manitoba, Canada

10   9   8   7   6   5   4   3   2   1

To Ralph

CONTENTS

CONTENTS

❋

ACKNOWLEDGMENTS

*T*he quest to find the book inside of you can be wrenching. Valued friends have invested precious time, prodded and persuaded, all to convince me that indeed there is something like that within me. If, dear reader, you too believe there is, then we have these trusting, farsighted people to thank: My husband, Ralph, who has been nudging me for years and doing my chores so I could write; our children, Shelly and Kent, who have provided much of the raw material, read the manuscripts and given their permission to include material about them; my sisters, Ardeth and Shirley, who give me confidence beyond my abilities; my dear, merciless friend Elizabeth Haglund, who never minced words or feelings when my talks or writings gave her a headache; Krista Halverson, my friend and editor, whom the Lord sent when Elizabeth moved on to edit heavenly writings; and the Great Encouragers at Deseret Book, led by Sheri Dew, Emily Watts, and Jana Erickson.

INTRODUCTION

*L*ongfellow said, "Into each life, some rain must fall," and what an inspired weatherman he was. It may be the only forecast guaranteed 100 percent accurate for everyone. The sister that you assume "has it all" is a fellow passenger on this ride of mortality. She has rainy days too.

Rain has a bad reputation. A symbol of misfortune, it is often associated with melancholy and suffering and misrepresented as a defect in the way life should be. But any farmer can tell you: If there's no rain, there's no growth.

As I reflect on the vivid experiences of my mortal education, I feel I am walking through a rainstorm—sometimes muddy and sometimes clean and refreshing, but never quite picture-perfect.

Never, unless I decide to look at my life as though it were rain on a flower garden.

Foliage relishes rain even though its life-giving shower often taxes the stems and leaflets. Following the rain, blossoms are washed clean and colors are more vivid and brilliant. Flowers raise their glistening heads on stronger stalks.

In life we experience both gentle showers and sudden and boisterous cloudbursts. The attitude with which we embrace them and the beauty we find in their unpredictability and necessity will determine whether or not we have the courage to venture out in the rain again.

I am grateful the Lord has loved me enough to send rain and allowed me to be able to walk in it, muddy and sticky or clean and refreshing. Each storm provides opportunities to grow up and the joy of splashing in some lovely puddles.

Come, dear reader, and walk in the rain with me. We will laugh and cry together. (And, if we're lucky, we'll get our feet a little wet.)

ALL RAIN, NO MUD

*R*ain in a town of paved streets and sidewalks is quite wonderful, an experience that still makes me marvel, for something renewing and invigorating happens when clean, fresh water falls from heaven without making mud.

The streets of my hometown turned to mud when it rained, cars splashed in it, and your boots got stuck. After the rain stopped, the mud often stayed for days.

I loved the rain but not the mud.

I discovered there is such a thing as rain with no mud only after I was married and we moved to the city—Utopia! From the moment our first child could walk, she had boots and a raincoat. Together, Shelly and I splashed in puddles, followed leaves floating down gutters, squinted our eyes, and stuck out our tongues to catch a few drops.

Rain was a reason to celebrate, that is, until Shelly started school. I didn't think it was a good idea to get her out of school in the middle of the day after my work was done, to walk in the rain. But I had an idea. I asked her, "How would it be if I walk you to school every day it rains?" Shelly hoped it would rain the first day of school. It didn't, but on the mornings when I had meetings to prepare for, appointments to keep, and errands to run, it rained. Mother Nature seemed to be saying, "Let's just see how serious you are about keeping your promise to a child."

I left breakfast dishes on the table, postponed errands, and rearranged schedules to keep my promise. Cars filled with school children stopped to offer rides, but we were building memories, and I was keeping a promise. We reveled in our rain ritual for seven years. Then came junior high school. I woke up one rainy morning and hurried into Shelly's room. "We get to walk to school today. It's raining."

"Mom, I can't," she said. "We're having a dance after school. But would you drive me so my hair doesn't get messed up?"

❋

Drive her I did. I was sad those walks were over, but glad we had them when we could.

Other rituals replaced the walks in the rain. The early morning drives to high school for cheerleading practices were informative rituals for me. At 6:00 A.M. I picked up three other cheerleaders and we drove to the school. If I was able to resist speaking (or "lecturing," as my children call it), reminding them that a mother was present, I was able to learn about Shelly's friends, her teachers, her worries, her plans—things mothers wonder and worry about but are not always privy to. I stored this information away for future reference.

Shelly grew up and began dating, so a late-night ritual was added to the early-morning one. (Rest homes are for parents whose children eventually leave home so they can get some rest!) Home from a date, Shelly would come into our bedroom and whisper in my ear, "Mom, I'm home. Come and talk to me." What she really meant was, "Come and listen to *me* talk!" I'd climb out of bed, carrying my blanket and pillow into the bathroom, and lie on the floor. While taking off her makeup and brushing her teeth and hair, Shelly would review every detail (well, *almost* every detail, so I imagined) of the events of the evening—who said what, and what she thought about it, while I lay there half awake, half asleep. There were times when I wanted to jump up and say, "You did *what?*" but sleepiness is a good friend at times like this. Once more, keeping quiet kept a mother informed. I knew I could sleep when she went away to college.

She did go away to college and eventually away to a family of her own. When I see her walking in the rain with her children, I hear her voice from the past, asking me, "Mom, how can I get my children to love the rain?" And every time it rains, I relive those glorious days of walking in the rain with my little girl.

101 USES FOR A RED CARPET—OR, AT LEAST, THREE OR FOUR

She was the kind of daughter you dream of having: compassionate, smart, friendly, appreciative, and beautiful. And now she was coming home after serving an eighteen-month mission for the Church. How can you show a beloved child just how much her life has added to your own? Balloons and signs were not enough. There had to be some way to say, "You are beyond wonderful. Thank you for all the joy you bring us."

Six weeks before her arrival, we were on the "countdown." I was watching the ten o'clock news. Queen Elizabeth was coming to visit President Reagan at the White House. When she stepped out of the limousine, the queen stepped onto a red carpet that stretched from the curb to the steps of the White House. That was the answer! A long, red carpet for our "queen!"

But I soon learned there is no such thing as a long, red carpet, at least, not one I could afford. I began to visit carpet stores, talking to every person in the carpet business I could find. Sales people looked at me incredulously and said, "You want WHAT?" They'd shake their heads and tell me, "Ma'am, if you want a fifty-foot carpet, you will have to buy fifty feet of carpet that is twelve feet wide. That will cost about $750.00."

Now, I love this daughter, but I also love thrift! (My children call that being "cheap.") Seven hundred fifty dollars to say, "Thanks, we love you"? There had to be some place I could find a carpet remnant. I continued my search, explaining my purpose and its importance, to any carpet person who would listen. But time was running out; our daughter would be home, and I would be left with only the welcome mat to greet her.

Late one Saturday night I ventured into a small carpet store. The manager was getting ready to close for the weekend. I told him my dream. He began with what I had heard so many times before, "Ma'am, I am sorry, I don't have a piece like you are looking for." Then he stopped. "Hey, wait a minute." His eyes lit up and so did my hopes. "I do have a bright, red remnant that is six feet wide and twenty-five feet long. We could cut it in half and tape it together, then you'd have a carpet three feet wide and fifty feet long."

I resisted hugging the man, but I did give him a high five.

Our missionary came off the plane. She had been flying for twenty-two hours and still looked better than I had ever remembered. Her eyes radiated light and goodness. The familiar blond, curly hair framed her beautiful face, and my precious, little girl was at last once more in my arms. My love and gratitude that the Lord would trust me with such a person to be my child was beyond my comprehension. I was right. She was a queen. I wanted to freeze that moment and the way I felt, forever.

Driving home from the airport took an eternity. I had to keep swallowing and taking deep breaths. Nothing could surpass the moment of seeing her at the airport, but the matter of the red carpet was approaching quickly. We were talking and laughing all the way home, but inside, my heart was pounding with anticipation. As we drove up the street she saw the Christmas lights strung from delphinium poles.

"What are the lights at our house?" she asked. By the time the question was out, she saw. The lights and friends and neighbors lined both sides. Tears welled up in her eyes as she got out of the car and walked home on red carpet.

"Welcome home, Shelly! Welcome home!"

Words couldn't come, only tears and hugs. She hugged and greeted dear people who had loved and supported her, not just for eighteen months but for her whole life. The red carpet had already paid for itself a thousand times over.

I remember trying to explain to my husband why this red carpet was so important. I said, "We will use it for more things than we can foresee right now, I just know it."

Since Shelly's homecoming, the red carpet has been in constant use. It is magic. It turns an ordinary occurrence into a celebration and elevates celebrations into extravaganzas!

Each of Shelly's babies has been welcomed home from the hospital on that same red carpet, stretched from the parking lot up two flights of stairs to a student apartment. The babies don't care about the red carpet, but the parents do. Mothers of missionaries living within a fifty mile radius have asked to borrow the carpet. Their missionaries return back to the home they left behind, on a red carpet.

Prom dates, marriage proposals (complete with horse and

❋

knight in armor), and wedding receptions are a part of the carpet's history. Its most poignant moment began with a call from a mother who had heard about the red carpet and its legacy.

"My son left home three years ago," she began, "I have not known where he is or if he is still alive." Her voice softened and then broke, "He just called and asked if he could come home." Hesitantly she asked, "May I borrow your red carpet?" That request alone validated the carpet's purchase. In fact, seven hundred fifty dollars would not have been too much to pay!

The red carpet has permitted me to play a small part in people's lives—parts that to them are significant and deserve celebrating. Each story that comes back with the carpet tells me one more time, if you really look, you can find reasons to celebrate someone every day.

BROKEN DREAMS

*F*or most of us, life hasn't turned out the way we dreamed it would when we were fourteen. At least mine hasn't. I've wondered if we set ourselves up for disappointment with illusions that can never be realized.

What we expected from life when we were twenty is irrelevant in the face of reality at forty or sixty or eighty. Relationships, health, and finances are all relatively manageable and uncomplicated during life's prologue. When we are young, days and years ahead hold hopes and dreams and excitement. In my mind's eye, I could see a wonderful husband, an idyllic life, free of complications and disappointment, and eight perfect children who in my mature years would rise up and call me blessed.

The thought that our lives would be anything but exhilarating and joyous was never even considered. What could possibly come into our lives that we could not handle? After all, I did have a wonderful husband and our first child seemed practically perfect.

That was the time I should have been called to teach a parenting class, or write a book on parenting. I had all the answers. I remember sitting in church watching parents struggling with active, noisy, rambunctious children, while I sat enjoying my quiet, demure little daughter. I knew what *I* would do if my child behaved like the ones I saw!

When I would observe teenagers acting out or straying from the path laid out by faithful, conscientious parents, I knew exactly what *I* would do if it were my child!

The Lord called my bluff! And, may I say to those of you who have yet to experience the adventure of teenagers, don't judge. Don't ever say, "When my child is a teenager, I am going to . . . whatever."

Our number two child has taught me more than I ever wanted to know, but I would not want to give up, nor ever give him up. It wasn't until he came along that I realized how naive, intolerant, and judgmental I had been. As if to validate our challenge, our bishop once told us, "Everyone in the ward has an idea of what you should be doing to raise your son."

One night our boy was angry with us and used model airplane glue to seal my husband, Ralph, and me in our upstairs bedroom. He glued the door frame to the door and filled the hole in the doorknob with glue. We heard a noise and got up to see what was happening. There was no way the bedroom door would budge. While I was thinking of tying bedsheets together and climbing out the window, Ralph was eyeing our clothes chute. It opened in our room and also out into the hall. It was about twelve inches by eighteen inches. Smaller than Ralph.

Do you remember the story of Winnie the Pooh visiting Rabbit in his hole and eating so much honey he got stuck in Rabbit's hole, trying to get out? That was Ralph, trying to wriggle his body through our clothes chute to get into the hall. He finally made it. We were no longer held captive, but our hearts were sad.

Experiences like this stripped me of pride, ego, and hastiness to judge. A friend said to me, "Sharon, you have no ego." I said, "When you raise teenagers, that is the first thing that goes."

That same son and I now laugh about the time I told him

I wanted him to wear a sign that read, "I have been taught better," and he said, "You make the sign, Mom, and I will wear it."

One day he left home in anger and told us we would never see him again. For two and a half long years we didn't. We only knew where he was because he occasionally called his sister. Every other month, I mailed his favorite cold cereal to him. The postage cost more than the cereal.

Over a period of forever, we have healed some open sores, and we are all continuing to work on the hidden wounds. Fear relentlessly creeps into the corners of my faith and withers my soul and my senses. I ask myself questions that have no answers. "Why do parents who appear to me to be less invested in their children, have responsible, contributing, and appreciative offspring?" "Why can't our son see the consequences of his choices?" "Why does life seem unfair?" "Why do experiences have to be excruciating before I learn?" "Why does life have 'diminishments'?"

There was a time when I was so emotionally welded to this child that it was difficult to tell where I ended and he began. Each choice he made dictated my next move, and he knew it. A wise friend helped me see. She said, "You are giving him a lot of power. He makes his choice and your choice bounces off his."

Words are easy. How could I stand by and watch him self-destruct? How could I face each day when my heart was broken? I had to muster up the courage to open myself to possible difficulties ahead, to be sure I was getting what I wanted out of life. I had to be careful not to lose faith that I would prevail (which I must *never* lose) while at the same time taking courage and discipline to confront the brutal facts of reality.

Either from weariness or desperation I came to realize I was not helping him or me by being a reactionary mother. I had to take control of my thoughts and my motives. When some days feel harder to bear than I can endure, I have to remind myself that our son has his agency given to him by God for a purpose— a God-given purpose—and I trust God. Then I stop and ask myself, "Why are you feeling so sad or discouraged or depressed?" If it is because of choices my son is making, I have to let it go. These are the hardest exercises of all:

To let go because the world does not need one more dysfunctional human being; and to hold on because, above all the pain, he can't feel abandoned. He must know I love him!

—— ❄ ——

The disappointments and shattered illusions tear open my soul and expose raw, vulnerable nerves. Tears come without warning, and I cry out, "What did I do wrong?" Then, instead of dwelling on unfulfilled dreams, I have to make myself create new ones, easy ones, fun ones. I have to keep checking to be sure I know who I am and who I am not. I am not an appendage of my son. My rest, peace, and happiness must not hinge on his choices and behavior. My relationships with other people I care about do not fluctuate with his behavior. He does not define who I am: This is on a good day.

My broken dreams do not mean that I am broken. I pick up the pieces with faith, hope, and above all, charity. I will not only endure but flourish—not in spite of the dashed dreams but most often, because of them.

DOING IN LOVE WHAT I LOVE TO DO

*S*ervice. The very word often brings to mind drudgery, necessity, dogged duty, and inconvenience. With the best of intentions our world has nearly wrecked this good, solid word. As those things that are "virtuous, lovely, or of good report or praiseworthy" seem to be losing favor around us, the concept of being of service has also fallen on hard times.

We've all heard the phrases "service project" spoken with ridicule on one side and "look out for Number 1" shouted with relish on the other. Any notion of removing ourselves from center stage is largely viewed by the modern world as archaic and unsophisticated, making service a pejorative exercise.

To me, unadulterated service remains synonymous with love and goodness and pleasure. Yes, pleasure. Haven't you found that when you experience something joyful and fulfilling, your first impulse is to share it? I have also discovered that shared joy need not be complicated. It can be as simple as rice pudding.

Recently I came across a recipe for rice pudding that is so delicious I wanted to share it. I checked with people over fifty years of age who I thought would enjoy my new dish. I made notes: Rulon doesn't want any raisins in his pudding; Joe and Heber want lots of raisins; Ruth can't have any spices in hers. When I first started this "rice ritual," I hate to admit I thought I was pretty wonderful and clever, customizing and making a treat for so many people at once. I made the basic rice pudding and then divided it up into separate, disposable cartons and customized the pudding according to taste.

I was out making my deliveries one day when I realized I had completely forgotten about my own "wonderfulness" and was actually having fun. I enjoy cooking and this gave me an excuse to cook more than I would eat and also an opportunity to visit with some people I was not confident enough to just drop in on to visit. I discovered that the nicest and most joyful way to serve is to do in love for others what I love to do—like riding in convertibles.

Convertibles are another passion of mine. Growing up in Canada made them totally impractical; living in Utah, only partially impractical. We finally got one and I wanted to drive it with the top down year-round. One Christmas I noticed horses pulling carriages around Temple Square so people could see the lights. Of course!

I called some of my friends who I didn't think would have a chance to see the lights on Temple Square. Kem had Parkinson's disease and couldn't get out. I arranged to pick him and his wife up, and we drove into town, stopped the car, and put the top down. We bundled them up in warm, cozy blankets, turned the car heater and the Christmas carols on full blast, then drove around to see the lights. At traffic lights, happy shoppers and children stopped to greet Kem and wish him a Merry Christmas. Although he was enjoying the experience, I was ecstatic! I had found a way to use this wonderful convertible in the wintertime too!

I thought next of Barbara. This was just the kind of adventure she would love. I was right. Barbara is handicapped. At that time she was my visiting teaching companion and brought her pure spirit with her every time we visited our sisters. Although

Barbara cannot speak, she can giggle and laugh, and her eyes can sparkle. The giggling started when the top of the car started folding down behind her. Her eyes peeking out of the blankets matched the bright, twinkling lights against the dark sky. Preserved in my memory is the sight of this beautiful woman overflowing with joy as we drove down the streets ablaze with lights and decorations on every building, tree, and lamppost. Could this be service when I was having so much fun?

In the spring, after visiting the exquisite gardens at Thanksgiving Point several times, I realized Glenna needed to see them too. No one I am acquainted with knows flowers like Glenna knows flowers. She not only knows their names, but she can see and point out the uniqueness that makes each one beautiful. I love the times she calls to say, "Sharon, you have to come this minute and see this daylily. It will never be more beautiful than at this moment!" I rush the half mile to her home, and Glenna tells me why this moment for this flower is its apex. Then we walk around her gardens and she tells me about the other flowers that will be coming along and promises to call me when they are at the peak of their crowning glory.

When I took her to the gardens, it was like seeing them for

the first time. I saw more and felt more than during any of my previous visits. Experiencing the gardens through Glenna's eyes and witnessing her passion for beauty brought new appreciation to me for God's creativity and generosity, and also, gratitude for giving me such a generous friend.

Giving service is not drudgery or dogged duty. It more closely resembles finding selfish pleasure. Selfish because I am doing what I love to do, and pleasure because it's shared. Sharing the ordinary, even sub-celestial pleasures with others helps me come alive—for surely I am re-creating myself when I gain a new friend.

GLENWOOD, ALBERTA, CANADA— POPULATION: 250

⁓ ❊ ⁓

*I*t was not your typical LDS church meeting in Hong Kong in the late 1980s. Attending were two General Authorities and the Young Women General President from Salt Lake City. At the conclusion of the meeting, one curious brother approached the three visiting authorities. "I noticed in the introductions," he said, "that all three of you are from the same place in Canada." Then he stepped closer and asked, "Just how big *is* Glenwood, Alberta, Canada?"

The implication of that question continues to be an anomaly. What is it that produced such a concentration of future Church leaders per capita in the Canadian and Mexican colonies? Was it isolation? Was it a controlled environment? Was it the hardiness of the settlers and their progenitors?

Curiosity about this phenomenon has caused me to snoop around my hometown of Glenwood, trying to pick up clues from my childhood. The answer is not easily discovered. For those of us who grew up there, our lives felt very ordinary. An outsider might have described our lives there as "simple," "sparse," or even "deprived." If we were any of those things, we didn't know it.

There were in fact extraordinary opportunities for growth in our little community—more than we could appreciate at the time. But looking in the rearview mirror, which casts a rosier glow with each passing decade, I see how those opportunities helped define us as we grew up.

Glenwood is an obscure little village nestled in the shadow of the Canadian Rockies, not a town you would ever happen on by accident. We loved it there and claimed all the meadowlarks sang, "Glenwood is a pretty little town."

In the 1940s and 50s, Glenwood ran like a well-structured private school. Its two hundred fifty occupants consisted of a perfect ratio of mentoring adults to growing children and young people. The adults pretty much all held the same values and believed in their children. It was a world where time and space were abundant and members of the rising generation were allowed experiences that helped us begin to discover who we were and who we were not.

The folks in Glenwood were not connoisseurs of extravagant living, but they had ways of loving life. Monday, Wednesday, and Friday the mail came, unless it snowed hard. This connection with the outside world broke the changelessness. Tuesday was activity night at the church, and every Thursday night we had a movie brought from Cardston, twenty miles away. Whatever the movie was, we watched it. We never felt our lives were short on adventure or narrow on exposure.

There were haystacks to climb and ditches to float leaves in and water skeeters down, rivers to swim in, and old barns to explore for new baby kittens. We often walked a block down the street to the cheese factory, Glenwood's claim to fame. Ned Davidson would dip into the huge aluminum vat and give us handfuls of delicious, rubbery cheese curd. We stood at the vat and ate to our hearts' content. Filled to capacity, we'd walk over to the vat of melted wax used to cover the large rounds of cheese and dip in our fingers. We loved to feel the soft, warm wax on our fingers. Ned knew our routine and let us practice our ritual each time we came.

But Glenwood wasn't Camelot. The winters were cold and long. I remember digging down through mounds of dirty snow in March to see if there were any sprigs of green grass, any evidence that spring really would come again. The wind was also a constant on the prairie. We had a saying, "If you hold a crowbar out in the wind and the crowbar bends, the wind is too strong to go out."

Good or not-so-good, this was our life as we knew it. We children assumed everyone in the world lived like we did. But the older citizenry saw something more. They saw future in the rising generation, and they invested in it.

From my earliest memory, I can see my grandma and grandpa, whom we called "Mama and Papa Leavitt," together with my aunts, uncles, and cousins on that side of the family, gathered in one big room in their home. Whenever we were together Mama and Papa Leavitt wanted a talent show. That was a misnomer! The younger cousins watched the older ones play their instruments, sing their songs in harmony, do their acrobatics, and dance. We knew the day would come when it would be our turn. Everyone clapped and cheered for any effort, regardless of quality or talent. This flagrant, unreserved attention fanned the flame of confidence in us.

Weekends usually meant some kind of party or dance or program at the church. To us, that meant performance. My sister Shirley, our friends, and I were the first to volunteer. Our unbridled confidence was not founded in long hours of rehearsal nor abundant talent. But the results were like the exhibit at Mama and Papa Leavitt's. Adults crowded the wooden church benches to watch the youth perform and encourage their investment. Their cheers and whistles validated our efforts, filled us with confidence, and sent us home preparing for another program. Every community event—weddings, church socials, funerals, or soldiers coming home from the war—provided another excuse for a performance and additional exposure for those who were willing to share their talents, as minimal as they might be. We volunteered our services for everything and they were accepted. It never occurred to us that we weren't any good. After all, we had the applause and cheering as proof. Our mentors and cheerleaders never told us we couldn't do it.

I was just thirteen years old when I was asked to play a pump organ for church, something I had never done before. It took hours of practice with patient singers, but I learned to play the organ. I wondered why Alice Nelson wasn't asked. She had been our ward organist for years. She already knew how to play.

One summer our church choir director and organist left town for summer school. My fifteen-year-old sister, Shirley, was appointed the choir director and I, at sixteen, was the organist. The thought that we couldn't do it never entered our minds, and the adults never missed a choir practice.

This was a community where performance was encouraged, confidence was nourished, and cheerful acceptance was standard. These farsighted adults consistently gave us the impression we were significant, and we believed them. So the next time someone asks the question: "Just how big *is* Glenwood?" I have the answer: "It is big enough."

GROWN-UPS—THEY COULDN'T DO WITHOUT US

My sister Shirley and I waved good-bye to our parents and headed off for college. We worried how they would ever survive without us. For most of our young lives we had worked in Mom's general store, driven the tractor on the farm for Dad, taken care of the animals, and cleaned house. In our minds, we did it all. As a matter of fact, we did do it all, especially when Mom and Dad would leave every April and October for the States to attend General Conference in Salt Lake City.

Looking back on those days, I see a level of trust from our parents we did not recognize nor appreciate at the time. They gave us opportunities for new experiences before we expected or asked for them.

When Mom and Dad left for the week, we opened the store promptly at 8:00 A.M., after feeding the turkeys and pigs on the acreage behind our house. We kept the store open until 6:00 P.M., or later if someone was still shopping. We knew the combination to the safe and opened it every morning and locked it every night. The thought of sleeping in or taking time off or pilfering money from the till, or even expecting money for our help, never even crossed our minds.

By the age of eight, I was routinely called to write my name on government checks, witnessing the marks made by Indians doing business at the store. I would carefully write my name in cursive as large, impressive Indians hovered respectfully, watching my work. I remember feeling quite important and even powerful that these big men needed my signature to cash a check. The odors of buckskin, tobacco, and campfire were always present. The Indians watched patiently, their long, black braids falling on the paper. On each check, I meticulously drew my name below an X made with the trembling, unsure hand of the Indians. This opportunity didn't last into the next generation when the Indians began sending their children to school.

Indians received checks from the Canadian government for

the use of their land. On mail days—Monday, Wednesday, or Friday—Indians rode into town on horseback or in wagons stuffed with children, the women wrapped in blankets to keep out the heat or the cold, depending on the season. They picked up their checks at the post office then crossed the gravel road to Mom's store where they retrieved the collateral they had left: beautifully beaded buckskin jackets, gloves, and moccasins in exchange for the checks.

The experience of working in Mom's store made me think I was an essential part of its operation, as did the responsibilities I was given on Dad's farm.

Barely big enough to see over the dashboard of Dad's old farm truck, I felt I was one of his more important farmhands as I navigated the truck through the hay field, which lay strewn with hay bales waiting to be loaded on the flatbed behind the truck. Dad and the hired help threw the bales, and I drove the truck. Dad obviously thought I could do the job, so I was determined not to disappoint him and to be the best truck-driver-baler-picker-upper he'd ever had. I had to slide down in the driver's seat to get my feet on both the clutch and the gas pedal at the same time.

This presented the problem of not being able to see over the dashboard. When the signal came to move to the next stack of hay, I'd take a quick glance at my route to the next stop for any big rocks or ditches I needed to miss, then I'd disappear behind the wheel to get the truck in gear. Gradually I'd let out the clutch and press the gas pedal with the tip of my toes, stretching my whole body as far as I could in order to see out. Then we'd lurch forward to the next pile of hay.

Dad could have driven the truck more easily, but I wasn't big enough to haul the hay. My ability, which was only as good as my determination and effort to drive, made one more person available for the heavy work. Dad needed me, and being twelve years old, I saw the task more like fun than work.

I also drove the tractor to plow fields, mow, and rake hay. I drove in my swimming suit because a dark tan was the pay for my summer's work. One day a blade on the mower broke and Dad sent me into town to get it fixed. Waiting while the blacksmith repaired the blade, I passed the time with the local farmers who were also waiting for their equipment to be repaired. We were peers, exchanging news of the day, speculating on how many cuttings of hay we would get that year, and sharing what grains we had planted and how the crops looked. We talked about the weather and wondered if there would be a long enough season to reap a good harvest. I was one with those farmers in the blacksmith shop and left with a mended blade and feeling very grown up.

I hear twenty-first-century parents complain that finding ways of empowering children today is difficult. In grandma's day, maintaining a livelihood required everyone in the family to participate. Validating children wasn't even in their vocabulary; it came about naturally and in the course of everyday events. Today it is difficult to legitimize child labor when machines do the work. It is also difficult in these times of plenty to simulate poverty and give children the opportunity to pay their own way. Some parents, in their efforts to help their children become self-reliant, appear either stingy or selfish.

Busy, self-contained parents who are concerned about efficiency and saving time can unwittingly cause their children to feel like a nuisance or an inconvenience. Helping a child discover and recognize his or her own personal power and unique gifts takes creativity and an inordinate amount of time. The effort is rarely efficient, but it is the quest of every caring parent.

My sister Shirley's oldest son, Lincoln, was fascinated with machines from the womb. Whenever a repairman came to the house, Lincoln was at his elbow, peppering him with questions. The clothes dryer, the dishwasher, the car—each held wonderful mysteries for Lincoln to unravel. When he was in his teens, he remembers the clothes dryer quit (with eleven children in the family, of course it quit!). His mother went to call the repairman, but Lincoln said, "Mom, let me try. I think I can fix it." Shirley wasn't sure she was ready for a dismantled dryer. "I really think I can fix it," Lincoln begged.

This had not always been the case. His mother often said she didn't think Lincoln would live long enough to put together all of the things he had dismantled.

"I've watched the repairman work on this dryer dozens of times. I know it inside and out." With wet laundry piled to the ceiling, Shirley took a deep breath and said, "Okay, son, give it a try." When she finally heard the hum of the dryer, she realized that her "witness after the trial of her faith" had arrived. Lincoln became the repairman. Anything that needed repairing, Lincoln was on duty, and he knew it.

By the time the floor of the family's old station wagon rusted out, Lincoln had added welding to his repertoire of skills. He remembers getting a piece of sheet metal to fit the hole in the flooring of the car. Riding in the car and seeing the road moving under your feet was disconcerting and precarious. Lincoln's dad was a busy stake president and working hard to keep a family of thirteen people afloat, so his mother offered to help him. She crawled under the car on her hands and knees, holding the sheet metal on her back while Lincoln welded it in place. Shirley was eight and one-half months pregnant at the time, and she didn't know how to weld, but Lincoln did. He, too, worried how his family would manage when he went away to college.

Lincoln is a dad now, and his seven-year-old son, Nate, can change a tire, rotate the tires, and change the oil in the car. Lincoln says it takes at least four times as long to do a job with Nate, but the investment in the future is worth it.

So is stacking dispensable dishes on the lower shelves of the cupboard so your four-year-old, who is still young enough to want to help, can empty the dishwasher. Asking your newly licensed driver to be the first driver on a family trip makes her feel not only important but trusted. Offering before she asks is where the power lies.

It is children (our own or other people's, nieces, nephews,

and neighbors) who enlarge our understanding, stretch us beyond our ability to grow on our own, liberate us from selfishness, and create within us someone we like. It's true. We could not survive without them.

HARD LESSONS

*T*aking the stairs down into the bowels of New York City is an almost surreal experience. Desperate to catch the subway you can hear pulling into the station, you race with your Metrocard in hand to swipe through the turnstile before someone rushing off the train tries to leave through the same turnstile.

Riding a subway in New York City during rush hour is an experience everyone should have at least once. Ralph and I were "lucky." For eighteen months we got to experience this phenomenon twice a day, every day, during rush hour. We lived on 66th Street and took the 1 or the 9 train down to 14th Street to our Public Affairs Office.

During rush hour, it appears that everyone in the city is leaving the subway and coming up for daylight. But wait, not everyone. At second glance, you see "everyone" is actually on the train you are hoping to catch. Its doors open for a split second, and you are either in or out. When the doors open and no one gets off, you know you could soon be wearing someone's cappuccino, because the guy drinking his morning coffee can't reach a pole to steady himself. I call it "The Sardine Run." You manage to squeeze in far enough for the doors to close and stay closed. Riding the subway during rush hour is for neither the faint-of-heart nor the hesitant traveler.

It was a day such as this when I caught a glimpse through the standing bodies of what looked like empty seats. Could it be? At the next stop, people shuffled and changed positions. I could see a man stretched across three rare and high-premium seats, sleeping! Two questions came to mind: How could he be sleeping with bodies teeming around him and, if in fact he was sleeping (which I doubted), how could his conscience allow it? Yet, he slept on. As new people squeezed on at each stop, they eyed those coveted seats and the man who held them captive, but no one spoke; instead, they cast sideways glances, shrugged their shoulders, raised their eyebrows, and frowned.

On 50th Street the subway lurched to a stop and a young man

boarded. In a matter of seconds, he had sized up the scenario and squeezed toward "Rip Van Winkle."

"Hey, buddy!" he said, tapping the snoozer on the shoulder. "Nap time is over."

The napping nomad jumped up swinging. "Don't you hit me!" he shouted.

Our hero calmly said, "I did not hit you, sir."

"Yes, you did!"

The atmosphere in the subway became brittle and uneasy. No one moved, but eyes were riveted on the drama. The young man spoke, "Sir, if I hit you, I am sorry. Please forgive me."

It was magic. Six words transformed the tense feeling in the train. The six words: "I am sorry. Please forgive me," delivered us from the suffocating fury we had fallen victims to.

The angry man slumped back down uncomfortably straddling two seats. Our liberator occupied the vacated seat, and we rumbled on our way in silence.

Introspection seemed to take over the subway. People asking, "What just happened here?" "Why did it happen?" "Was there something I should have done?" The penetrating anger of one person made the ride unpleasant for everyone. "Have I ever made others uncomfortable because I became angry?"

Ah, there it was. Yes, I have. And it all came back, even though it had been twenty years.

I had taken some family photographs to a studio to be enlarged for Christmas gifts. The studio assured me they would be completed in time to mail for Christmas. On the day they were to be finished, I took our nine-year-old daughter, Shelly, with me, and we drove to the studio to pick up the photographs. The clerk said, "I'm sorry. Your pictures will not be ready for another week."

When I heard that news, I could feel anger welling up from my toes. Let's just say I was irritated, quite irritated. And I let the clerk know how I felt about it. "You promised! I have to mail them to Canada!" I blustered. I took Shelly's hand and stomped out of the studio, trailing a black cloud behind me.

I was still fuming as we drove home, repeating in my head my tirade in the store, trying to justify my anger and my behavior. I looked over at my precious little daughter. She was strapped in her seat belt, staring straight ahead. What was she thinking of her mother, the one the Lord was depending on to guide her and show her how to live and behave?

By the time we reached our driveway, I was penitent and ashamed. "Remember, Sharon," my brother-in-law used to tease, "you can always serve as a horrible example." There was no doubt at this moment; I had indeed been a horrible example! When we got inside the house, I said, "Shelly, I behaved very badly in the photo shop. I have to go back and apologize to that sales clerk." (This was the *last* thing on earth I wanted to do. It was late. The shop was thirty minutes away, and I was embarrassed.) "Before I go," I continued, "I need to ask Heavenly Father to forgive me and to help me. Would you have prayer with me?"

Her face lit up and she said, "Would you like me to say the prayer, Mom?" I think after what she had witnessed, she wasn't sure I was yet in a state of mind or spirit to pray.

Holding hands, we knelt together by our couch and Shelly said, "Heavenly Father, my mom has made a mistake. Please forgive her and bless the man in the store to be kind to her. Amen." We hugged and, fortified by the prayer of my precious tutor, we returned to the store. My heart was pounding as we waited for the clerk to finish with a customer. (Humility is not easy medicine.) As we waited, Shelly said, "I'll just wait for you over in the corner. You can do it, Mom!" and off she went, leaving me to slay my own dragons. *Wait a minute,* I thought, *who is the mother and who is the child here?*

Finally the clerk I had offended was free. I gulped hard and walked to the counter. He did not look pleased to see me. I had rehearsed all the way back to the store what I would say. But it was harder to say aloud, "I owe you an apology for my behavior. Will you please forgive me?" His face softened, and he too seemed relieved of a burden. Shelly's prayer was answered: the clerk was kind and forgiving.

It was a miracle. The sledge hammer that had been pounding on my heart was gone. It was easier to breathe. I even noticed the sun was shining outside. Shelly came over smiling and took my hand as we walked to the car. Driving home again, even the car seemed lighter and easier to manage. I knew why: We were carrying no baggage.

REFLECTIONS ON STYLE AND SUBSTANCE

*T*imes Square has style. Times Square, New York City, *invented* style—the kind of colossal, sensory-numbing spectacle you have to experience to believe. In that location, every conceivable form of media has been gathered and activated to grab your attention and your money.

The message comes through clearly (to me!): I have "been weighed in the balance and found wanting." I am not thin enough, young enough, pretty enough, or rich enough.

Walking down Broadway I see a blinding, pulsating assortments of LED screens wrapped around 30-story buildings, displaying the news, broadcasting the NASDAQ market averages, portraying scenes of surfers and snowboarders, and showing movie trailers. The visual noise echoes through emblazoned marquees and into the night sky, demanding your attention.

Saturating the senses further is the aroma of roasted coconut, pretzels, and hot dogs mixed with the smell of cigarette smoke, diesel fuel, and horses carrying policemen. Then the sounds of the city reach your consciousness and you are aware of honking taxis, squealing bus brakes, the chatter of innumerable languages, including varying forms of English. Techno music vibrates through the air and clashes with the rhythms being beaten out on empty, plastic detergent buckets, played for break-dancers. A circle forms around the dancers and foot traffic comes to a standstill.

Welcome to Times Square, New York—The City That Never Sleeps—The Insomniac, where *less* is going on than meets the eye.

Sometimes I have become so mesmerized with the style that I don't stop to ask myself, "Wait a minute! What is *really* going on here?"

In my travels abroad, I have seen style in all its configurations. Different religions each have their own unique styles. I once witnessed the celebration that accompanied the completion of a new church building, which was heralded on several Jumbo-trons and by the music of a big band dressed in bright yellow suits playing hip-hop music. Confetti filled the sky when the ribbon was cut to open the new building.

In one city I was privileged to attend a special church service of another faith. Strains of Bach from a pipe organ filled the rafters of the majestic cathedral. Church officials wearing elegant robes and colorful headgear formed a procession up the long aisle. Their movements were choreographed to every detail and their script was precise. Gold adorned the altars, candelabras, and other accessories. My British heritage reveled in the pageantry, the style.

But my mind could not resist returning to another church service in Novosibirsk, over the Ural Mountains and three time zones east of Moscow, deep in the hub of Siberia. We climbed three flights of steep, metal stairs that were clinging to the outside of an office building. The room was small and cold and dark, except for one dim lightbulb that had been brought and screwed in for the service and which would be taken out after the meeting to await the next service. A small table and about twenty metal folding chairs were the only furnishings in the stark room.

When we began singing, a miracle happened. The room became warmer and brighter because we were singing together about the same Savior, the same prophet, the same covenants. Sacramental prayers in a foreign tongue felt familiar because I was worshiping with my brothers and sisters. Solid gold goblets and platters would have been compatible with the richness I was feeling in my soul as I took the bread and water from a small chipped plate and a tiny paper cup. Why did this uncluttered, unaffected, straight-forward service reach my reaching? Why did I find myself looking around expecting to see angels among us? There was much more going on than I could see.

The sacred covenants we make and the ordinances we celebrate in our Latter-day Saint meetings and temples eclipse anything this world can offer, but sometimes those kindred feelings I felt in Novosibirsk of belonging, peace, safety, and home come when I walk in Central Park. A new adventure awaits Ralph and me every morning as we walk in the park—new streams, a new stone bridge, a moss-covered archway, bird-watchers with their binoculars poised, the changing seasons, the stone steps leading to a secret garden, the fragrance of nature at work, sounds of birds and water and wind in the trees.

Evidence of God's handiwork anchors me. God's perspective comes closer here because nature obeys God. I am surrounded by obedient spirits. The seasons do not capriciously change their rotation. Ground squirrels don't decide one year to hibernate in the summer. The sun doesn't change its course in the universe.

In Central Park I am rescued from self-absorption—worrying about my shape, my hair, my clothes, and how others see me. Souvenirs in abundance proclaim God's love and link me with God's creations.

I never tire of watching the ducks and geese swimming in the lake, leaving tiny wakes behind them. I can watch the colored leaves reflected in the water day after day, and watching the sun rise over the trees never bores me.

Just give me what is real, what is true, and what is good, and my soul will take a deep breath and smile. Novosibirsk or Central Park will do.

SECOND BEST AND STILL OKAY

*O*ne of the first barbs that penetrated my young skin was an amazing discovery: I was not number one! Report card day documented the dreaded evaluation that there were people both younger and smarter than I. I was average, a status I had never considered in my young life. This first brush with reality came when my younger sister, Shirley, and I brought our report cards home the same day.

Because we attended a small country school (read: *Little House on the Prairie*), we were in the same school class taking the same subjects. Mom and Dad sat down with us and scrutinized every section down through the teacher's comments that unfailingly read, "It is a pleasure to have Shirley in class," and "Sharon would do better if she talked less."

Shirley was not only smart. She was smarter than I was, and still is. I knew that if I spent the rest of my life studying, I would still never be as smart as Shirley.

This experience with report cards and Shirley started me thinking about myself, not as I had always believed me to be, but as others saw me. Who was the real me, anyway? Neither my parents nor my siblings saw me as a lesser human being. I had not fallen from acceptance or love at home.

I struggled with my own form of schizophrenia until high school where I began to trust my own instincts about myself. It happened in gym class.

Every week the teacher chose two team captains for a volley-ball game. The rest of the students lined up against the wall to be chosen on the teams. As the captains called out their names, the students left the wall and stood by their captain. Shirley was usually one of the first to leave the wall, then everyone else, except me. Invariably, every time, I would be left standing alone by the wall, the last one, not even chosen—just left over, and feeling worthless and embarrassed. Each week I prayed that I would not be the last one chosen, even second to last would have been better. But each week it was the same.

❊

What saved me from total despair was the discovery at the ripe old age of fifteen or sixteen that "I do not have to be a volleyball player to be a worthwhile and contributing human being."

This newfound revelation released me. I still felt embarrassed and awkward standing to the last. But the truth was, I could not play volleyball. I wouldn't have chosen me if I were the captain. However, the truth also was, playing volleyball was nowhere on my radar screen of interests or ambitions. Volleyball was not who I was. Why pick up a problem I didn't have? While I stood against the wall and others were chosen, I tried to list the things that were me: "You have lots of friends who like you, you do all right in school, you can play the piano and accompany people who sing, and you have a family that thinks you are spectacular." Telling myself what I *could* do helped me survive the humiliation for what I could *not* do.

This important discovery about myself, made in high school, gave me the mettle to handle a pivotal experience in college.

My date and I were going to the homecoming dance and double-dating with another couple. During the evening, it was my friend's date to whom I was attracted. He was charming, fun, and cute. He was also tall and blond with captivating dimples.

I was ecstatic when he called me the next day, but my ecstasy plummeted when he asked, "Would you get me a date with your roommate [Mary Jones]?"

The old feelings from volleyball rejection erupted once again, and in a pique of irritation, I heard myself saying, as evenly as I could muster, "You know her. If you want a date with her, call her yourself."

I was smart enough to know this man was worth knowing, and I was determined enough not to just hand him over to some other girl. I was obviously not number one to him, but he didn't know the me I had known for twenty years, or at least the last five years.

Life went on, but I would often find myself thinking about this tall blond with dimples. Then a telephone call came for me while I was in Bountiful, Utah, spending Christmas vacation with my older sister, Ardeth, and her husband, Heber Kapp. I heard this vaguely familiar voice saying, "Hi! Do you remember me? I'm Ralph Larsen. We double-dated at Homecoming last year."

Did I remember him?!

"There is a Christmas dance next week. I was hoping you might go with me."

I wanted to say, "Where have you been all this time?" but I took a deep breath and tried to sound casual, "Oh, sure. That would be fun." After hanging up the phone, I screamed my joy to anyone who would listen, "I've got a date with Ralph Larsen!"

Time together and time apart, letters and phone calls, eventually brought this dear man into my life forever. I am grateful I had the confidence not to set Ralph up with Mary Jones.

It has taken a while (Kolob time, maybe seventy-two minutes; earth time, some fifty years) to reconcile myself to the fact that my significance and happiness does not depend on how much the world values me. Even though my task is to improve each day, it is possible, even desirable, to be at peace with who I am in a world where the bar for "best" is raised daily.

But the need to prove myself persists. My sister Ardeth became a well-known Church leader and author. Her name was a household word in our locale and abroad. I grew used to being called "Ardeth Kapp's sister." This was not difficult for me because I love her, and she has always been my cheerleader.

Then came a new acquaintance, and again, a healthy dose of reality. She was younger and smarter and a woman who was on the way up. My world rearranged itself, and in our assignments in the Church, Sheri Dew and I covered several continents, several times, spending days and nights and airplane rides together. Now, before you become covetous, let me describe what it is like to travel and work with Sheri. It is probably how it would be traveling with Jennifer Lopez, with slight differences in wardrobe. We would get off the plane and it would start. Women who have seen Sheri on television or read her books, would rush up, calling, "Sister Dew! Sister Dew!" They wanted to shake her hand, get her autograph, and have their picture taken with her. Since I was left standing around doing nothing, I would often become the photographer.

As heady and ego-inflating as you think this might be for Sheri, she doesn't get it. She honestly doesn't fully understand the impact she has on people and the blessing she is to so many of us. In spite of her talents and abilities, she continues to view herself as just "a simple farm girl from Kansas."

On one of our trips, after she had once again been the center of attention, she turned to me and said, "You know, Sharon, I am always the bridesmaid." I could see my chance, so I said, "Give it up, Sheri! All my life I have been Ardeth Kapp's sister and now I am Sheri Dew's traveling companion. *I* am the brides-maid, not you!"

The question constantly presents itself, "How can I love people who are so superior to me?" And then I go back to the volleyball days and think about the things I like to do and the things I can do well. I can make mouth-watering dinner rolls, I can listen empathetically to a friend. It feels natural for me to hug people and reassure them of their value. These specific, unique gifts allow me to borrow confidence from my authentic self. Trying to keep my covenants, attend my meetings, and stay close to the Lord delivers me from the pain of enduring the world's judgments. I am rewarded with relief and release, know-ing the Lord accepts me, even while the tests continue.

Being second best is not just okay; it is liberating and free of pressure and a whole lot of fun—kind of like the donkey who ran in the Kentucky Derby. He didn't win the race, but he was on the right track, and he ran in great company!

SLOW GROWING

*W*hat should a young wife do when she discovers that her husband is not perfect? How does she recover from this unsettling, even heartbreaking realization—when the idyllic and romantic days are replaced with reality, paying bills, and the demands of rearing children? Why can't marriage go on as it is for newlyweds forever? Why can't agency go on holiday while the children are teenagers?

There were bumps along the early way for us but no major potholes or, if there were, I don't remember them. The realization that my husband had some major flaws only came to me about twenty years into a good marriage, while we were trying to raise our second child, a son. This is a story of discovery and recovery.

At the beginning of marriage, relationships appear to be uncomplicated. Newlyweds face life with more hopes and dreams than worries and responsibilities. Before them stretch days and years of happiness and fulfillment.

Up until we had our second child, life, marriage, and children were relatively predictable. We braved poverty as students and infertility as newlyweds. Then by a miracle, after five years, our daughter was born, and it appeared that life would just keep getting better. We attended symphonies and ball games. I taught school, Ralph went to school. He gave me a guitar and lessons and washed the supper dishes while I practiced "Red River Valley." He tended our daughter before his morning classes while I taught early morning seminary. I found other activities and experiences to keep me involved while Ralph studied and studied year after year. We were a smooth-running team. Life was better when we were together.

Just when we assumed the road of life would always be a smooth highway with green lights ahead, a big yellow caution light began blinking in the form of child number two, born ten years after our first.

Because of newfound difficulties, we began feeling our

marriage wasn't like it used to be, and we resented having to change our ways and what had always worked in the past. We wanted things to be "the way they always had been."

It is no secret that life changes for everyone in the family when a child becomes a teenager. Our marriage experienced major trauma when our teenage son chose an alternative road, one not being traveled by the family. His insistence on following a contrary path introduced contention into our marriage and into our family. Fearing what might become of him held our happiness hostage. What had previously been viewed as mere idiosyncrasies in my husband and me were magnified into major annoyances. Previous insignificant weaknesses in character seemed to grow into enormous hurdles overnight. Intolerance and suspicion began to raise their ugly heads in our relationship.

As our son grew, so did the stress and conflict. We were three individuals (our daughter was away at college), who loved each other but who each had a different perspective. We limped along, my husband and I trying for some kind of peace or contentment or at least consensus in how to help our son.

It didn't always work. We discovered that trying to raise a child when the mother and father hold differing philosophies and beliefs is a minefield in marriage. My husband and I had been raised under entirely different parenting techniques. Ralph's training had been *casual* with high expectations. Mine had been *controlled* with high expectations. Both methods seemed to work reasonably well, at least for us. Then along came our son whose behavior challenged our parenting philosophies and our marriage. My husband's laid-back attitude caused me to think, "Well, somebody has got to step up here," and I became more controlling and manipulative out of sheer fear. The more frantic I became, the more Ralph backed off, to balance this foray. Ralph and I were accelerating in opposite directions, away from each other.

The whole thing bubbled to the surface when our son was in his early teens. Our stake youth were preparing to perform a wonderful musical production called *Cumorah's Hill*. I knew this was the answer to my prayers. If we could only get him involved, I felt certain it would make a difference in his rebellious attitude. The words to the songs of truth and goodness would get in his head, and he would be involved with righteous young people and leaders who loved them.

I was determined that our son *would* participate, and I set out on a campaign to get him excited about it. My husband took me aside one day and said, "You know, Sharon, it will be much more effective if he *chooses* to be involved. Coercion and bribery are not going to make this the kind of experience you are hoping for." I knew what Ralph said was true, but what if he didn't choose what *I* wanted?

Our boy couldn't understand at his young age, I reasoned, how influential and powerful this kind of experience could be in shaping the rest of his life. I needed to step in and take charge. He would thank me in days to come that he was among those four hundred youth who would be singing:

> We'll love, and learn, and overcome;
>
> We'll sing a joyful song,
>
> As Zion's youth in latter days,
>
> Triumphant, pure, and strong.
>
> (*Hymns,* no. 256)

He participated all right. He went to the practices and sang the songs. But, as Ralph had warned, the words went through his head but not into his heart. It was just one more disappointment, but I felt it keenly. Our home was not a refuge from the storm, it *was* the storm. We knew the Lord understood our broken hearts.

We knew He loved us and our son. It was a pivotal moment for us. We knew that this trial could either strengthen or weaken our family and our marriage.

As a couple we prayed together each night before our private prayers, asking for understanding and patience with each other and our son. Each fast Sunday and every Friday was a special fast day for us in behalf of our boy. When times became especially difficult, my husband would give me a blessing of comfort. And, once, our home teachers gave Ralph a blessing.

It was humiliating and excruciating to admit that we had a problem that appeared to be bigger than we were. However, our need was greater than our pride, and we eventually contacted a professional counselor who was also a trusted friend.

To go to this counselor was the first thing Ralph and I had agreed on in months. We were hopeful he could help us navigate the stormy sea that was threatening to destroy us. Our friend helped us understand that though our son was doing things that were wrong, Ralph and I were not perfect either. The counselor told Ralph he needed to step up as a dad and husband, and he told me to "chill out" and quit being a "control-freak." He didn't use those words, but we understood. He told me that when I was tempted to lecture, I needed to go into the bathroom and lecture the towels.

Stretching and straining away from old tried-and-true-traditions, letting go of obsolete behaviors that once worked, trying to understand the child and what the spouse is feeling, admitting past mistakes and supporting a new plan, is the most exhausting work spouses and parents can do.

After we had been given some insight and developed the courage to make needed changes, we were on the road to recovery. It was a stressful process, and we will never again take our marriage and relationship for granted.

We continue to pray privately and as a couple. Temple and Church service strengthens us. We have to work every day to be patient as we wait for understanding to evolve. We are not the same couple that started out forty years ago. We certainly don't look the same, and we hope we are wiser.

There are still bumps along the way, even potholes, but together our shock absorbers are working better than ever before—and I am still trying to understand agency.

THE FIRE-EXTINGUISHING BUSINESS

I called my companion to see if she could go visiting teaching on Tuesday. She said, "Oh, no, I couldn't possibly go on Tuesday. That is the day I clean my oven."

Another sister refused to participate in any extracurricular activity until the scrapbooks of her five children were up-to-date.

In a former life, I would have laughed at these excuses. Cleaning an oven? Children's scrapbooks? Where do they fit on a list of priorities? Certainly not on my list of "significant ways to spend your life." I would have pulled out my planner and shown those sisters what "busy" really is. Back then I believed the world would go into meltdown if I stopped to clean my oven (I had a self-cleaner) or complete a baby scrapbook. Want proof? My twenty-six-year-old has yet to see his.

There was a time when I felt confronted from every angle—by my housework, my Church work, my children, my husband, and the need to care for my aging parents. The list was bottomless. I was in over my head and snorkeling to breathe. The demands and expectations were beyond my ability to perform. Surely no one else's life was as hectic or relevant as mine.

How did I cope? Well, when the "over-burdened-under-able-syndrome" hit, I could either show off or complain, or do both. I noticed I could justify my agitation by reciting my schedule and deadlines to someone: the meetings, the speaking assignments, the lessons to prepare. This soliloquy seemed to validate me. After all, I had places to go, things to do, people to meet!

This was my unconscious pattern until one day, years ago, when Dad stopped by to see the children. He casually asked, "Well, Sharon, how are you?" It was like a fire hydrant had been opened. I took off on a tirade, with my planner in hand, showing and telling Dad how busy I was and how much in demand I was. "And look at all my appointments for just today," and, "besides all that, Ralph has invited his office staff for a Christmas dinner, and I am chairman of the ward Christmas party."

Dad dutifully looked at my planner and listened to my

recitation. When I finally quit venting and stopped to take a breath, he sat thoughtfully. I waited, anxious to hear praise for all I was doing from this man I loved and respected with all my heart and soul.

Dad had an 8th grade formal education and a Ph.D. in perspective and wisdom. He got up from his chair, came over, and hugged me. Then he looked me straight in the eyes and said, "You know, Sharon, it doesn't take much to keep some people busy." Then he left.

He didn't get it. Busy? *I* was the definition of busy! What was he talking about? Was he insinuating that I was *not* busy? I had my planner and schedule and demands to prove I was not only busy, I was important. And why should I feel defensive—even angry— at what was only an insensitive and obviously unenlightened response from my dad?

Shortly thereafter, I was visiting a dear friend whose common sense and insight I respect. I took the opportunity to also give her a rundown of my life and what I was doing with it, as though it were as significant to everyone else as it was to me. Just as my dad had, she listened patiently. Then she said, "It takes some kind of arrogance to think you can accomplish all those tasks with any kind of effectiveness."

Arrogance! That word sent me home thinking. What was I doing with my life, and was I simply stroking my ego by taking on all the things I was trying to do? Was I in the fire-extinguishing business, going for the highest flames regardless of what else was burning around me? Was my calendar being filled with my ego and insecurities or with honest priorities?

In my ripening years, I see every twenty-four hours as an incredible gift. Being busy is not a negative, and I am not a victim. I have a choice. I want to be all used up when I die, but at peace with what "used me up." Who am I to judge the sister with the clean oven or the mother with the completed history of each one of her children? Those sisters accepted the choices they made and they knew why they made them. I am not competing with them.

It is an exciting pursuit to discover who you really are, deep down inside, and then consider the choices that made you that way. When my peace is at war with my planner, I check my motives. I have learned that when my motives are grounded in my own interests or ego, it doesn't take long for life to become flat. I become weary, even in well doing.

When I was called to a demanding Church job, the president told us: "This calling will take a great deal of your time. You cannot expect to just add it to everything else you are doing. You will have to let some of your previous activities go." This was an important lesson for me to learn—to let some things go, to determine the "weightier matters" for me. I had to quit singing in a wonderful professional choir where I enjoyed the music and the company. It was important to me, but not as important as other commitments I had made, such as to my family.

The epiphany came when I noticed that my activities and involvement could exhilarate me. I had a choice. I could choose to live deliberately and consistently with what I valued, independent of outside pressures. This paradigm has energized me and given me confidence and permission to choose. I have never been sorry that I let the phone ring while I read bedtime stories to our son or while we were eating dinner as a family. I have never been sorry for the times I walked in the rain with our daughter, or arranged my schedule to be home when the children came home from school. An appointment with my husband is the most important appointment I make, and I keep it. I have missed book clubs and dinner groups, luncheon engagements and symphonies, for higher commitments.

This is what I have learned: I can be in control of my life. I can leave the dishes in the sink while I visit a friend. I can drop everything and go see a budding daylily when it is at the peak of its beauty. I can listen to a teenager and try to understand her heart. The house does not need to be spotless before friends come to visit. I don't feel guilty, because these are choices I make about my time and my priorities. I find pleasure in small things. When I clean the refrigerator, I keep opening the door to see how good it looks. I even like a clean oven! I am grateful when I remember a friend's birthday or write a note to someone who gave a thoughtful, soul-stirring lesson. (I wish this occurred every day!) But when I live centrifugally, there is more zeal, exuberance, and downright fun in living!

Dad was right. It doesn't take much.

THE VIEW FROM
DIFFERENT TOWERS

*O*ne morning, during our customary walk in Central Park, Ralph and I noticed a woman coaxing her dog to "fetch." She threw the ball and it rolled along the sidewalk. The dog stood like a statue looking at her as if to say, "Are you crazy? *You* fetch it!" So the owner obediently ran, got the ball, and threw it again, repeating the same routine over and over, she running after the ball and the dog stoically looking on.

As we continued our walk, we saw another woman intent on the same activity, with greater success. She was more rotund than the previous dog owner. She threw the ball and her dog took off after it, bringing it back in short order. In the interim, the owner would have strolled about three steps. Again she threw the ball and again the dog took off.

❉

The presence of dogs in the city is an absolute anomaly to me. My rural rearing makes it difficult for me to fathom the reasons for keeping an urban pet. New York City dogs wear customized cloth coats with matching booties and coordinated collars and leashes. Their owners carry plastic bags and little shovels to take care of what the dogs leave behind. My country memory says, "That is the epitome of misguided use of energy, time, and even affection!" Dogs are dogs, not people.

I've heard it said, "If aliens came to New York City and tried to convene a meeting with the dominant species, they would see people going around after their dogs picking up poo and quickly conclude that dogs are at the top of the social order." The top of the social order for pets, maybe.

The line between pets and people becomes blurry in the city. My life in Manhattan collides with my former life on the farm. With "country" in my bones, living in this energetic, exhilarating, never-stop city is an adventure in perspectives, a view from a different "tower."

Steel mountains that pierce the sky are home to eight million people. My friend, a New Yorker, took her daughter camping upstate. She wanted her six-year-old to see trees and space and unobstructed blue sky and even see the stars at night. They were gone for three days. As they drove across the Brooklyn Bridge and back into Manhattan, the little girl cried out, "Oh, Mommy, look! There are my buildings! My beautiful buildings!"

Living in an urban setting, what I miss is the slow rhythm of life in a small town. Walking down a country road with dust covering my shoes, the smell of newly mowed alfalfa fields, and the beauty of the Rockies bordering the sky is about as close to heaven as I can get—no buildings, no pollution, no barriers—only rolling fields, majestic mountains, and blue sky big enough to fill the universe.

But now as I stand on a "city tower" looking over variegated landscapes and lives, this experience in the city adds abundance to my being. A brand-new view of the world brings me a brand-new view of myself, expands my sensitivity, and urges me to press for interpretation. What do dog owners see? What do city dwellers feel? It would enlarge my understanding if I knew. Then I dare to press further and ask, What does my son see? What does he feel? Why can't I stand on *his* tower and dare to look over *his* vista? Can't my love extend that far? For him? For us?

Eight years ago, when he was eighteen years old, my son

said, "Mom, I don't think I am ever going to serve a mission." I gulped hard, took a deep breath, and said, "Whether you serve a mission or not, I am going to love you." Then I ran to my bedroom, collapsed on the bed, and cried my heart out. His life, his perspective, his friends, his values have become foreign to me, even while I desperately fight to keep him close.

I have learned how not to dissolve at missionary farewells, but only until they sing the anthem for missionaries, "Called to Serve." The temptation to flee the meeting and retreat to my home in tears is almost irresistible, but I must stay grounded and secure so he will always know where to find me. The reach of my arms and my heart must stretch beyond his conforming or complying. It must encompass this stranger who is my son.

It has taken years for me to accept that he can choose in his way of life and his friends. Heaven knows he has had plenty of lectures and exhortations on those subjects! He knows my rote lectures by heart, but does he have any idea how much I love him? It is time for love and acceptance of a precious child of God. I can do it for acquaintances, and I am learning to do it for my son.

Tempering expectations for a beloved child is not easy, if not devastating, for parents who wish only the best for their children. As painful as lowering expectations is, it is not as lethal as the persistent disappointments that jar your emotions relentlessly. So the true test for me is to keep a one-sided relationship fluid, functioning, and even fun, without feeling inside like a martyr or a victim. It is a personal battle I have not yet won.

Patience and perspective are inextricably connected. The amount of patience I need depends on whose tower I am viewing life from. When I view dogs in the city, my supply of patience must be increased to see what dog lovers see. My "home" work is to see what my son sees.

On difficult days, it helps to think of another perspective.

There are times when I have been consumed with my own broken dreams and ready to quit or retaliate. I have felt unappreciated, hurt, and despitefully used. Then the Spirit whispers to me from yet another tower: "How many times have you taken from the Lord and never recognized His gifts? How many times has He carried your sorrows and pain and you have not understood? His love is extended all the day long. He may have to withhold blessings, but never, never His love."

It is a lesson I am still learning.

FLYING TOGETHER

*K*ent, what is your father's hobby?" asked our son's Scoutmaster. The fathers were being introduced at a Scout Court of Honor. Kent's response was immediate. "Model airplanes," he said. "We build remote-control model airplanes, and then we fly them."

This was news to my husband, Ralph. But he got the message: Kent wanted to build and fly remote-control model airplanes. Ralph said he had noticed the catalogues lying around the house and wondered.

Following the Court of Honor, Ralph and Kent began their new hobby, poring over catalogues and exploring possibilities for the aviation novice. Their workbench in the basement was directly below the kitchen, so I could hear their conversation.

Which airplane? Which engine? Which radio control? Which fuel tank? The decisions were endless, and father and son debated every option.

Our fledgling pilot became an enthusiastic laborer because model airplanes were not without cost. He mowed lawns, pulled weeds, washed cars. He helped repair the sprinkler system and even cleaned bathrooms. It felt like forever to Kent, but finally he had enough money to order his first airplane, the one he and his dad had agreed would be a good one to start with. Then came more waiting—this time for the plane to arrive.

When the FedEx truck finally pulled up, carrying a box with Kent's name on it, the box was snatched, opened, and assembly had begun before the FedEx man could get a signature.

The new hobby introduced our family to a whole new world. A world of airplane glue, exacto knives, paper, and paint. And there was balsa wood—lots of balsa wood—to be cut out, punched out, trimmed, and fitted for wings, fuselage, tail and motor mounts. And don't forget the radio control and levers that move elevators, rudder, and throttle. Our basement told the story: piles of paper with intricate instructions were stuck to each other with toothpicks saturated with epoxy glue. The iron, used to stretch and smooth paper over the wings, tail, and fuselage, had left its imprint forever on the arm of the sofa. Chatter, laughter, and groans of frustration leaked up through the heat vents from the basement, followed by long periods of silence. Much more was going on than building a model airplane. Finally, all the pieces fit and the shiny, new plane was ready for its maiden flight.

The plane was ready, but were its creators? This fragile structure of wood and paper and glue and metal had occupied father and son for weeks. Sure, it looked perfect. But unspoken doubts, questions, and angst intruded on the long-anticipated moment. Were the builders ready to take a chance and possibly lose their creation?

Neither had ever flown a remote-control plane before. People they had watched made it look easy. But it couldn't be. Radio controls are very sensitive. It must take hours of practice to really know how to fly. What if the unthinkable happened? What if it crashed?

Kent cradled the plane on his lap as they drove to the airstrip near our home. They had been there many times before, listening to stories and watching the techniques of veterans of the sport. The vocabulary that had sounded so foreign a few months before was familiar today.

The moment of truth was nearing, and father and son could not speak—their beating hearts were deafening. Kent carefully climbed out of the truck holding his prize. He set his plane on the smooth, hardened clay and started the engine. His dad held the throttle open while Kent adjusted the fuel jets to their maximum RPMs. Then the nervous pilot took the radio control and the copilot held the plane back, waiting for the signal from his son. After a few deep breaths and gulping hard twice, Kent said, "Okay, Dad. Let her go!"

The plane jumped off the airstrip into the air at maximum throttle and soared straight in the air. It looped around once before Kent leveled it off. A split second later it was in a nosedive, headed for sure annihilation.

The devastation on the ground was only exceeded by the devastation in the heart of a boy. Trying to hold back the tears, he ran to the wreckage. His plane, his time, his money, his confidence were shattered on the airstrip and nearby fields. Quietly father and son began to search for the pieces of their plane. Crawling through tall grass they found a piece of the tail.

Fuselage parts were found in the next field. Other pieces were lodged in rock piles or snagged in bushes.

When they had collected all the remains, Ralph could see that reconstruction was possible. He spoke the first words, "Kent, we can repair this plane and fly it again. We've got all the pieces. We are in the airplane business again!"

"Dad, do you really think it's fixable?" Kent's quiet voice didn't dare hope.

"Not only is it fixable, but that man flying his plane over there just told me that you could get a dual radio control box so he could fly with you. That way, he could help you until you learn how to fly your own plane."

Father and son hurried back to the basement, back to their glue, their toothpicks, and their balsa wood—and back to each other. The chatter, the laughter, the groaning from the basement was heard anew as once again father and son were flying together.

"IN THE MIDST OF AFFLICTION MY TABLE IS SPREAD"

$\mathcal{S}$acrament meetings are long for children to sit through, especially after they've already been in Primary for two hours. To keep her young boys pacified during that last hour, our daughter would bring treats for them. One Sunday they were sitting patiently, waiting for the sacrament to be over so they could have their goodies. As the tray for the bread was passed down our aisle, three-year-old Jake saw it coming and whispered in my ear, "Tell them we don't need that bread. We brought our own treats."

I had to admit, Jake was right. His treats did look more inviting than the plain pieces of broken bread. But what a three-year-old sees in the sacrament and what a covenant person sees in that symbol of blessings unimaginable, are impressions far removed from each other. Still, in a way, Jake and I understand each other. Sometimes what the Lord has in mind for me to see with His help is as difficult as it was for Jake to understand the broken bread. Too often, I think my idea is more attractive or even better for me than the banquet the Lord has prepared. It is hard to choose the Lord's banquet when there is a "mess of pottage" so easily at hand.

I couldn't see any banquet when I drove my dad back from the doctor's office where he was told he had stomach cancer and would likely live for only a few months. What was wrong with asking the Lord to heal the most perfect man I knew? Tears spilled down my face as I drove. I didn't want Dad to see. He didn't. He was looking out the window at the Wasatch Mountains and clear blue sky. He said, more to himself than to me, "I wonder what the Lord wants me to learn from this experience."

I couldn't be as philosophical. All I wanted was my dad to be well again. Just when I thought Dad had taught us everything, he taught us one more thing: how to face death with dignity and with faith. His favorite topic became his "graduation." He would tell us who he was going to see when he graduated and what he was going to tell them about us. He gave each of his children and grandchildren a blessing. Mom and Dad's last will and testament illustrated what they valued. The first page records their most precious possession and the one they wanted to leave their children: their testimony of the gospel of Jesus Christ. The second page of the will basically says, "Divide among yourselves what you want and take the rest to the dump." Dad was helping me learn about faith.

After Dad passed away, Mom came to live with us. More celestial aerobics. She had osteoporosis and could not move without a great deal of help. Our son Kent was almost three years old at that time. It seemed I was either taking Kent to the bathroom or Mom. When I'd get Mom bathed, it was time to bathe Kent. I would just get Kent fed, and Mom was hungry and needed help. I didn't know which end of life's spectrum I was living on. I felt like a martyr. Was this what Heavenly Father had planned for me? It wasn't feeling much like fun.

Then the guilt would set in, and I would feel worse than ever. So I'd give myself a talking-to and remind myself of all Mom had done for me in my life. I could not have had a better mother for me, and the guilt cut more deeply. How could I get out of this guilt-resentment-martyr-cycle?

I don't know if it was the blessings Ralph gave me or my fervent prayers or a loving Father in Heaven or all of the above, but eventually I realized this was my chance to grow up. I felt like the Lord was saying to me, "You know, Sharon, you were not the perfect daughter in your teens. I am giving you a second chance to make it up to your mother for those times you were thoughtless and inconsiderate of her." There were days back then I would like to erase and relive. That was not possible, but now I could be the kind of daughter I wish I had been back then.

Accepting and filling Church callings have likewise been an exercise in faith. Why in the world would the bishop call me to serve in the Relief Society when I had happily served all my life in Young Women? Didn't he know where I would be more effective, and by the way, where I would enjoy serving more? Fortunately, the Lord knew. The calling provided opportunities to serve my sisters and thus love them more, and it stretched me in different directions. I already knew how to give my shoulder to teenagers in Young Women to cry on. I could tell them with surety that most of their troubles would be over by next week.

Not so with my sisters in Relief Society. For some of them, I saw no end to their troubles. All I could do was cry with them. The faith and goodness of the sisters I worked with still strengthens me today.

The challenge of working with men in the Church has been another kind of education in trying to understand the Lord's curriculum for me. There have been times when I have wanted to say, "Just step aside, brethren, and the women will do the job." In fact, one good man I worked with said, "You know, Sharon, sometimes you come across like a bulldozer!" I would not have taken that remark so seriously if the man had not been the owner of a large construction business. He knows what a bulldozer can do.

Why does the Lord put men and women together when they think so differently? Could it be there are things I could learn from the men in the Church? Absolutely! The gentle priesthood holders who have patiently listened to me and taught me and helped me succeed are among my eternal blessings. We do see things differently, but often that is where the fun lies. It is broadening and invigorating to hear the perspective of someone who comes from another planet—like Mars.

Many a time I have started out to convince the brethren of some incredible idea that if they would all ratify, we could quit wasting time and get something done. As time and discussion, questions and input are offered, the wonderful idea is transformed. It becomes *our* idea, invariably better. It's simple: My "treats" are not as good as what the Lord offers.

My sister Shirley never gets confused about the difference between the Lord's treats and a mess of pottage. She and her husband, Ron, received a call from the area president. Would Ron serve as a counselor in the temple presidency? Ron's answer came immediately as it always has—"Yes," he would. Then Ron had some questions the temple president had to answer. Ron began, "You know, president, that I live across the border in Canada. Does this call mean that I will need to quit my dental practice?" The president said, "Yes, that is what it means."

Ron continued, "Does this mean that we will need to pay for a place to live in the States, near the temple?"

"Yes," came the response. "You will need to do that."

Shirley called me with the news. She was excited. I said, "Shirley, what is the exchange on the dollar between Canada and the United States?"

"Thirty-three percent," she replied, as though that was irrelevant.

I said, "So for every $100.00 you spend in the States you lose $33.00?"

"That is right," she said and laughed!

I said, "Shirley, how are you going to do this? Ron has to quit his dental practice and you have to pay for a place to live and the exchange on your money is thirty-three percent? Isn't that asking a lot?"

She said matter-of-factly, "The Lord knows our resources. We will be fine."

Staying home in British Columbia and keeping his dental practice certainly appeared more beneficial from a mortal perspective. But Shirley and Ron have never been encumbered with mortal perspectives. The way they saw it, now that their eleven children are raised, they would spend time together in "heaven" for three years. How do you put a price on that?

The poet said it,

> In the midst of affliction my table is spread.
> With blessings unmeasured my cup runneth o'er.

> (*Hymns,* no. 108)

Why do I think I know better than a loving Father who created me and knows my resources and abilities? For a little girl who grew up on the Canadian prairie with a high school graduating class of just ten people, the twists and turns my life has taken are beyond anything I could have dreamed. How could I have known what to ask the Lord for when I had no idea what was beyond the gravel road in my town?

The Lord knew. His banquet for me is spread with blessings unmeasured. My cup runneth over with gratitude for sacred covenants that bind me to Him and blanket me with love and hope and grace. When the Lord is my Shepherd, I shall never want.

*S*haron Larsen has served on the Young Women general board and in the Young Women General Presidency. She was born and raised in Canada, where she was in the top 10 of her high school graduating class. (There were 10 people in the class!) A graduate of Brigham Young University, she has been an institute instructor and has taught in elementary schools in Utah and Missouri. She also wrote, produced, and starred in programs for the Utah Network for Instructional Television.

She and her husband, Ralph, served a Public Affairs Mission in New York City. They are the parents of two children and four amazing grandsons.

Sharon's joys in life include her family, a good book, giving parties, and walking in the rain with people she loves.